12 WAYS TO GET A TICKET TO SPACE

WIDE EYED EDITIONS

HOW TO GET A TICKET TO SPACE

So, you want to follow in the footsteps of the first astronauts and **BLAST OFF** into space?

Good news! You were born in an era of great technological change, in which humankind is working on ways to travel into space like never before.

Rocket companies are launching cheaper, smarter, reusable rockets that land neatly on landing pads. New spaceports are under construction. Space agencies are preparing to send people to the Moon and Mars—and space tourists can reserve a seat on a rocket and dock with a space station just for fun!

It's never been so easy to get a ticket to space. Whether you're a daredevil adventurer, rocket-obsessed dreamer, a scientist on a mission, or a planetary pioneer, there's a place in space for you.

One thing's for sure: however you decide to go, the view from space will change the way you feel about life on our beautiful planet forever.

Which ticket will you choose?

CONTENTS

ASTRONAUT HALL OF FAME

Yuri Gagarin

First man in space. Completed one orbit of Earth in Vostok 1. 1961

Valentina Tereshkova

First woman in space. Completed forty-eight orbits of Earth in Vostok 6. 1963

Neil Armstrong

First person to set foot on the Moon. Commander of the Apollo 11 mission. 1969

Eugene Cernan & Harrison Schmitt

Longest stay on the Moon: 74 hours, 59 minutes on the Apollo 17 mission. 1972

Mae Jemison

First Black woman in space, on board *Endeavour*. 1992

Valeri Polyakov

Longest time living in space: 437 days on board the Mir space station. 1994-1995

James Voss & Susan Helms

Longest spacewalk: 8 hours, 56 minutes, to prepare the ISS for the installation of a storage unit. 2001

Jerry Ross & Franklin Chang-Diaz

Most spaceflights. Each astronaut launched in NASA Space Shuttles seven times and helped to construct the ISS. 1982-2002 and 1986-2002, respectively.

William Shatner

Oldest person in space, at 90 years old. Launched on Blue Origin's New Shepard rocket. 2021

Keisha Schahaff & Anastatia Mayers

First mother and daughter and first Caribbean women in space. Virgin Galactic SpaceShip Two. 2023

First person to pilot a homebuilt rocket into space

First woman on the Moon

First kid in space

First person on Mars

The Astronaut Hall of Fame gets larger every year.
One day, these milestones will also be reached—perhaps by someone your age!

FLY IN A SPACE BALLOON

You're on the launch pad before dawn, ready to float into a starry sky. The space balloon, lit with spotlights, is the height of a seventy-storey building. Attached to the balloon by a strong cable is a passenger capsule waiting for you to board. Inside is a comfy lounge with seats, snacks and huge windows.

You take your seat and, with a *whoosh* of gas, the balloon lifts off. You drift up at a gentle 12 miles per hour. As you rise higher, the towns below blur into spots and chains of light criss-crossing the land. You leave the troposphere, the thickest layer of the atmosphere, where most of the air is.

What is the atmosphere?

Earth's atmosphere is the layer of gases surrounding the planet. It protects life on Earth from the Sun's harmful rays and the coldness of space. The atmosphere is thickest near the surface of the planet, where gravity is strongest. The atmosphere thins as gravity becomes weaker farther away from Earth.

Launch vehicle: Space balloon

Mission type: Suborbital

Altitude: 100,000 feet

Destination: Earth's stratosphere

Time spent at the edge of space: About 2 hours

Total mission time: Around 6 hours

Ticket cost: $50,000–$125,000

The pilot tells you to look up. Millions of stars dot the blackness of space. Through the onboard telescope, you spot far-away constellations and swirling galaxies. You couldn't see these from Earth!

You float into the stratosphere, and from about 50,000 feet travel through the invisible ozone layer—a band of protective gases that stops life on Earth from getting dangerous sunburn. You look out of the windows, marveling at the colors of Earth, the peaks and valleys and brilliant blues of the ocean. You reach apogee, the highest point of the flight, and drift at an altitude of 100,000 feet. You call your family and take selfies in front of a view that stretches for almost 400 miles.

Look at me!

BALLOON FACTS

Balloon and capsule height: 400 feet

Balloon width (fully inflated): 330 feet

Capsule width: 16 feet

Seats: Six to ten people

The balloon slowly descends back into the troposphere and you drift through layers of wispy, billowing clouds. Then towns, rivers, and trees come into view and the captain asks you to take your seat for landing. With a hiss, giant cushions inflate beneath the capsule, and you land with a bump!

How do space balloons fly?

Space balloons are filled with helium or hydrogen gas. These gases are lighter than air, so the balloon floats. As it rises, the air pressure from the atmosphere decreases. This causes the gas inside the balloon to expand, which makes the balloon rise higher. Space balloons are launched part-inflated to leave room for this expansion. To bring the balloon back to Earth, the gas is released through flaps controlled by the pilot.

You climb out and look up. *"Now that was high!"* A car takes you back to the launch site for a celebration. Congratulations: you are one of the highest fliers in the world. Only a few people have stopped off in the stratosphere to enjoy the view.

RIDE ON A SPACEPLANE

After three days of safety training and health checks at the spaceport, you're cleared for take-off. You zip into your flight suit and stride onto the runway. Attached beneath a twin-hulled carrier aircraft, the spaceplane is unlike any plane you've ever seen. You climb through the hatch, find your seat and strap in. For now, there's nothing to do but relax and enjoy the view while the carrier plane taxis down the runway and takes off.

The plane flies to an altitude of 50,000 feet, higher than most people have ever flown.

"Three, two, one... Release, release, release!"

The spaceplane detaches from the carrier and DROPS.

MISSION STATS

Launch vehicle: Spaceplane

Mission type: Suborbital

Altitude: 270,000 feet

Level of atmosphere: Mesosphere

Time spent in space: 10 minutes

Total mission time: 90 minutes

Ticket cost: $440,000

Passenger planes fly at speeds just below the speed of sound: around 575 miles per hour. The space plane rockets to three times the speed of sound (Mach 3): around 1,980 miles per hour.

Your stomach lurches upward, for one, two, three seconds.

ROAR!

The rocket engine ignites. As the spaceplane maneuvers into a vertical ascent—straight up!—g-forces pin you to your seat, but you can still turn your head to look out of the window. The sky turns from blue to black. You see the curvature of Earth and the fragile layers of the atmosphere glowing against the blackness of space.

The rocket engine cuts off and the plane coasts up to 270,000 feet. This is your cue to unstrap.

11

Your body feels light as you push out of the seat. Your feet don't touch the floor: you're floating.

"Welcome to zero-g!"

NASA states that a person becomes an astronaut when they fly above an altitude of 26 feet.

It's surprising how easy it is to move. Below, snow-capped mountains glisten in the sun, rivers carve through continents and storm clouds bubble over the ocean. From the window, you can see for over 620 miles.

What are g-forces?

Standing on Earth, we experience a gravitational force, or g-force, of one. We are used to this force, so we don't feel it. But when we suddenly change speed or direction, such as when braking in a car, we feel a stronger force. When a spaceplane is accelerating, a passenger may feel a g-force of three. This force is strong enough to pin them to their seat and can also stop the free flow of blood around the body, making them feel dizzy.

Enjoying your last minutes of weightlessness, you fly across the cabin and do a somersault. Then the spaceplane glides back to Earth, the air thickens, and gravity returns you to your seat with a bump!

What is zero-g?

When a spaceplane cuts its engine and starts a controlled fall back to Earth, for a short while, the spaceplane's freefall counteracts Earth's gravitational pull. Passengers experience zero-g, also called weightlessness or microgravity, and float as if there is no gravity pulling them down.

The spaceplane lands gently on the runway. In the astronaut's lounge, you celebrate with family and friends. Then comes the moment you have been waiting for: the captain presents you with your astronaut wings!

BUILD YOUR OWN ROCKET

You've been building rockets since you were old enough to stack wooden bricks. After years of improved drawings, practice flights, and the odd spectacular explosion, your dream has come true. All being well, you will soon become the first person to pilot a homebuilt rocket into space.

The rocket stands on a launch platform floating in the sea. You thank the team for their support. Rocket fans from all over the world have given their time and money to help build and fly this rocket. But there's only one seat and it's yours!

"Comms—check!
Internal power on—check!
Flight software—check!
Navigation computer—check!
We are go for launch."

Inside the capsule, it feels like being locked in a tin can. Trying not to think about the highly flammable rocket fuel in tanks beneath your seat, you focus on the pre-launch checks with mission control.

MISSION STATS

Launch vehicle: 33-foot high rocket

Mission type: Suborbital

Altitude: 344,000 feet

Level of atmosphere: Thermosphere

Time spent in space: About 3 minutes

Ticket cost: Whatever money you can spare to buy parts for the rocket, plus your free time.

Your stomach does a nervous flip.

5, 4, 3, 2, 1...

Ignition.

The engines hiss and roar to life, sending vibrations through the capsule.

"We have lift-off."

Thrust is the force that pushes a rocket upward. When the thrust of the engines is greater than the rocket's weight and drag, the rocket will lift off and fly.

G-forces squish you into your seat as the rocket accelerates to Mach 3 and the sky turns from blue to black. After 90 seconds, the rocket booster cuts off and separates from the capsule, but you're going so fast that you continue to fly upward. Mission control cheers as you pass the 328,000-feet Kármán line. *You're officially in space!*

15

Earth is enormous through the porthole window. You want to stay for longer gazing at our beautiful planet, but soon the capsule begins to descend.

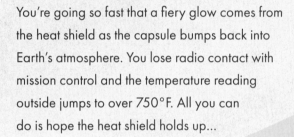

You're going so fast that a fiery glow comes from the heat shield as the capsule bumps back into Earth's atmosphere. You lose radio contact with mission control and the temperature reading outside jumps to over 750°F. All you can do is hope the heat shield holds up...

How do rockets fly?

A rocket lifts off by burning fuel and firing hot exhaust gases downward, which makes the rocket move in the opposite direction—upward! Engines in space work the same way. When a rocket engine is fired, the spacecraft moves in the opposite direction.

Rockets literally bump into the air as they fly, which slows them down. This is called drag. A rocket is designed as a smooth tube with a pointy nose, so it has a smaller surface to drag through the air.

When rocket capsules return to Earth, the flat side goes first. The drag on this surface slows down the capsule. Capsules can re-enter the atmosphere as fast as Mach 25—so fast that air becomes trapped in front and creates heat. The flat surface of the capsule is also a heat shield to stop the capsule from catching fire.

After a few nervous minutes, mission control is back on the radio. "Deploying parachute." With a jolt, the first and then second parachutes open and the capsule floats down for a splash landing. The recovery boat races to you and winches the capsule onto the deck.

Rockets have computerized guidance systems to control stability and direction. Sensors keep track of the rocket's movement and engine nozzles can be moved to change direction.

Congratulations! You've proven that with a lot of teamwork and effort, anyone can build and fly a space rocket.

WIN THE SPACE LOTTERY

It's your lucky day. The ticket you bought months ago has been drawn from thousands of entrants. You've won a seat on a spacecraft going into Earth's orbit. Not only are you going to be an astronaut, you're going to a top astronaut academy to train for your mission.

All your training and tests are completed and the weather is looking good. With the mission commander and pilot, you step into your specially made spacesuits and pose for photos. Then a car whisks you to the launch pad and you stand beneath a dizzyingly high rocket. You zoom up the elevator of the service tower and sign your name on the wall of the access corridor, a tradition for every astronaut that passes through this gateway to space. When you're strapped in, you give the thumbs up.

A rocket booster houses the engines and fuel needed to push spacecraft into orbit. When the fuel is used up, the rocket booster separates from the spacecraft and returns to Earth. Most modern rocket boosters are flown by computers and return to landing pads. They can be reused many times, making spaceflight cheaper.

3, 2, 1...**zero**

The rocket booster's nine engines ignite all at once, sending a brilliant flash of light through the window. You shoot up into the dawn sky. A few minutes later, the first-stage rocket booster separates and returns to Earth. Then the second-stage rocket booster ignites, propelling the capsule into orbit. You whizz around Earth at 17,400 miles per hour in a spacecraft that's only 13 feet wide—about the size of a bedroom!

MISSION STATS

Launch vehicle: 170-foot-high rocket

Mission type: Low Earth orbit

Altitude: 722,000 feet

Level of atmosphere: Thermosphere

Time spent in space: Three days

Ticket cost: $12.50 lottery ticket

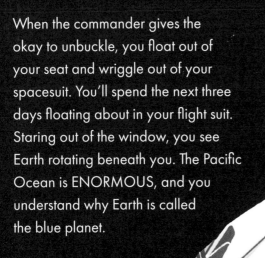

When the commander gives the okay to unbuckle, you float out of your seat and wriggle out of your spacesuit. You'll spend the next three days floating about in your flight suit. Staring out of the window, you see Earth rotating beneath you. The Pacific Ocean is ENORMOUS, and you understand why Earth is called the blue planet.

Few people have been to space, and scientists are still learning how it affects the human body. You record your heartbeat, sleep, and meals—and even when you go to the toilet! There's a foothold so you don't float away and a curtain for privacy.

You pee into a suction nozzle and poop into a 8-inch-wide tube that sucks everything into a storage bag—if you miss, it floats around the capsule! Everyone takes it in turns to sleep, snuggling into a sleeping bag strapped to the wall.

How do spacecraft stay in orbit?

If you throw a tennis ball on Earth, gravity will cause it to fall in a curve toward the ground. Orbiting spacecraft experience the same gravitational pull as the ball. The difference is that spacecraft are launched at extremely high speeds, and the curve of the spacecraft's fall is so large that it matches the curve of Earth. The spacecraft continuously falls around the planet, creating a circular orbit. Astronauts experience microgravity because their orbiting spacecraft are in constant freefall.

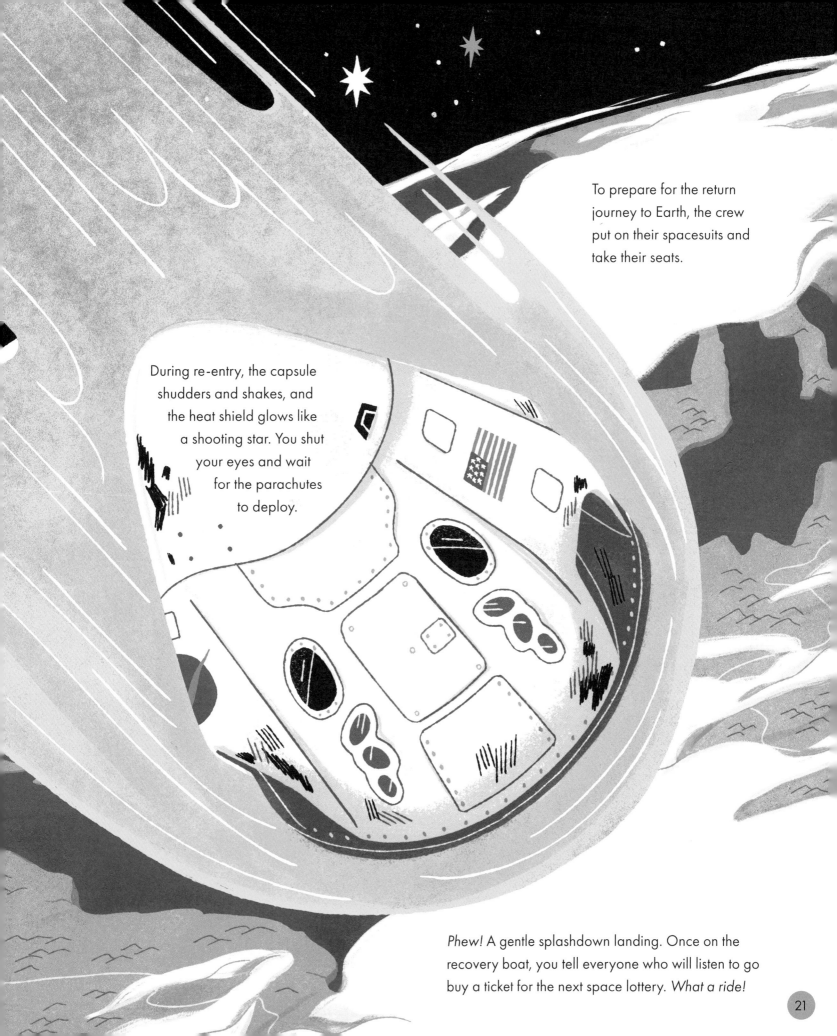

To prepare for the return journey to Earth, the crew put on their spacesuits and take their seats.

During re-entry, the capsule shudders and shakes, and the heat shield glows like a shooting star. You shut your eyes and wait for the parachutes to deploy.

Phew! A gentle splashdown landing. Once on the recovery boat, you tell everyone who will listen to go buy a ticket for the next space lottery. *What a ride!*

ASTRONAUTS IN TRAINING

Everyone who launches into space must complete some training to prepare for the demands and dangers of space travel. For tourists, this can take from one day to six months, depending on the spacecraft and journey. Pilots, engineers, and mission specialists train for much longer. Trainee astronauts are called candidates. They complete up to two years of general training. When they are chosen for a mission, they train for a year or more with their crew. But astronauts never stop learning: their job is to explore the unknown!

Welcome to the Astronaut Training Center

High-g

Candidates fly in a T-38 jet plane to experience steep climbs and stomach-churning turns to get used to the speed and changes in gravitational forces (g-forces) of a rocket's launch and capsule's re-entry into the atmosphere. A centrifuge machine tests how many g-forces a person can cope with. A capsule on the end of an arm whizzes around in a circle creating g-forces. Strong g-forces can be dangerous: they push blood away from the brain or heart, making candidates blackout.

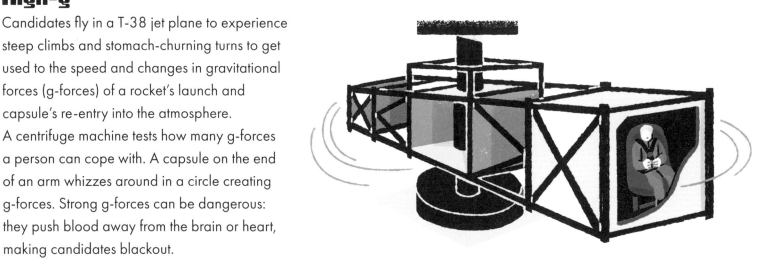

Zero-g

A specially adapted airplane nicknamed "the Vomit Comet" flies candidates in a series of up and down curves. Each time the plane glides up to the top of a curve and begins to fall downward, the candidates experience around 25 seconds of microgravity, also called weightlessness or zero-g. It's a flying roller coaster ride and makes candidates feel very dizzy and sick at first.

Moving heavy objects

In microgravity, it's easy to push a heavy object, but once in motion that object keeps going until it is stopped by a force equal to the one that moved it. Training centers have air-bearing floors. Air is blown through holes in the floor, creating an air cushion on which astronauts practice moving floating equipment, a bit like air hockey!

Splashdown!

Landing in water is the safest way to arrive back on Earth, but what if the capsule starts to sink before the recovery boat arrives? A candidate must complete open water survival training and be able to swim at least 75 meters and tread water for 10 minutes in their flight suit and shoes.

Top teamwork

Candidates go on survival training trips into the wild to see how they cope in a stressful environment and if they can work as a team. They also spend time together in caves or underwater research centers to practice living in an enclosed space.

Spacewalk

The natural place to practice weightlessness is in the water. Astronauts must first become qualified scuba divers. Training centers have deep pools with a model of the spacecraft on the bottom. Floating in their spacesuits, candidates practice spacewalks to repair and install new equipment.

Virtual reality

Life-sized models help astronauts find their way around spacecraft and rovers. Simulators teach astronauts how to operate flight and life-support systems and prepare for anything.

Talking to people on Earth

Everyone wants to know what it's like to live in space. Part of an astronaut's job is to share their experiences and discoveries with reporters and space fans.

Learn Russian

The USA and Russia are major participants in ISS operations. Astronauts and cosmonauts work alongside each other, and many of the controls are written in Russian.

BECOME AN ASTRONAUT PILOT

**As soon as you were old enough, you learnt to fly planes.
Now you're a top pilot who's studied aerospace engineering and completed
three years of astronaut training. You've been chosen to fly a scientist, an
engineer, and an artist to the International Space Station (ISS). Their safety
is your responsibility. Spacecraft are mostly automated, but a pilot must
know how to fly without the computer's help in case anything goes wrong.**

The ride up is a breeze. The booster engines separate, leaving the capsule
orbiting Earth. While your passengers admire the view, you check the flight
path. Over the next 4 hours, the thruster engines maneuver the spacecraft
into the same orbit and speed as the ISS.

You constantly check the capsule's telemetry with the ISS and
mission control. If you are off course or going too fast when
you dock, you'll bump into the space station, risking lives.

As you slowly approach the ISS, a robotic docking ring extends and locks onto the capsule. It pulls the capsule into the docking port, which tightly seals around the spacecraft hatch.

Docking is complete.
Welcome to the International Space Station.

How capsules fly

Sensors and cameras on the spacecraft record information such as speed, direction and distance. They send this information to computers on the spacecraft and space station, and to mission control on Earth.

MISSION STATS

Launch vehicle: 170-foot-high rocket

Mission type: Low Earth orbit

Altitude: 211 miles

Level of atmosphere: Thermosphere

Time spent in space: 182 days

Ticket cost: Zero! You are paid to work in space.

While you wait for the station crew to prepare the dock, you help each other out of your spacesuits. The dock has been open to the airless vacuum of space. Before the hatches are opened, the dock needs to fill with air and warm up. The space station commander also checks there are no air leaks.

The space station orbits Earth at a speed of 17,400 miles per hour. The station has its own engines but also relies on the engines of docked supply ships to move it into a higher or lower orbit.

Up to eight spacecraft can be docked at the space station at one time.

Finally, you get the all-clear to open the hatch and you float onto the space station where the crew welcome you with a hug.

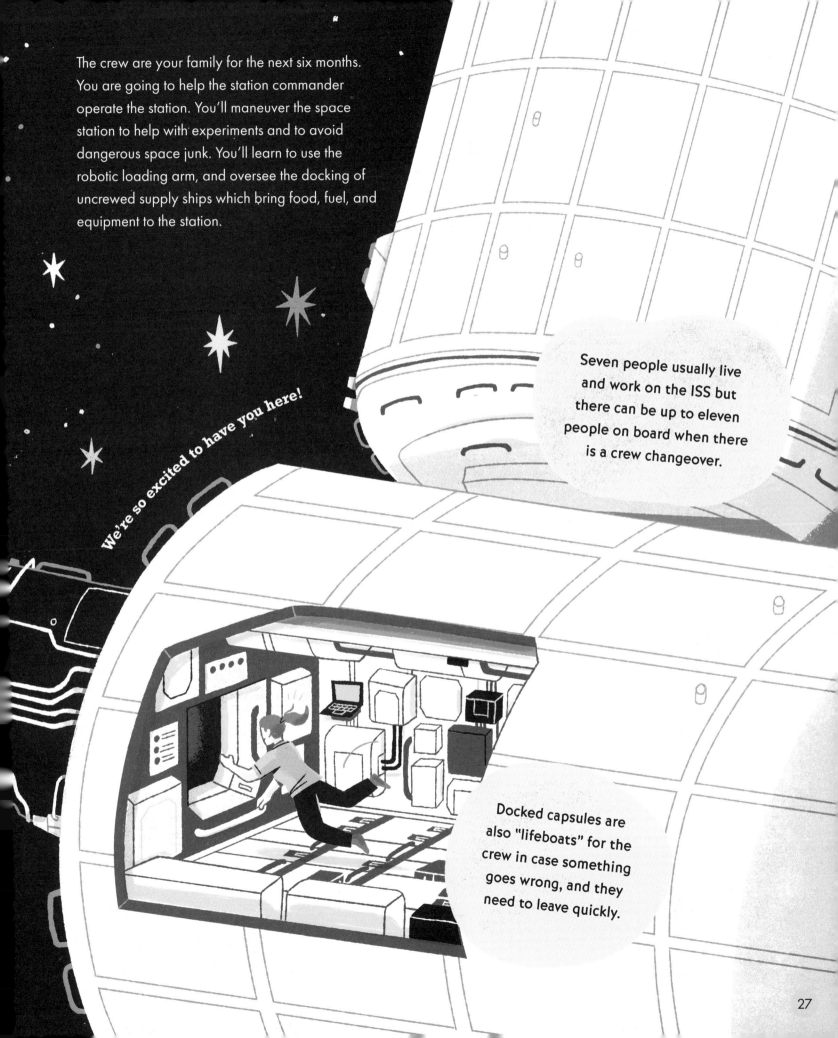

The crew are your family for the next six months. You are going to help the station commander operate the station. You'll maneuver the space station to help with experiments and to avoid dangerous space junk. You'll learn to use the robotic loading arm, and oversee the docking of uncrewed supply ships which bring food, fuel, and equipment to the station.

We're so excited to have you here!

Seven people usually live and work on the ISS but there can be up to eleven people on board when there is a crew changeover.

Docked capsules are also "lifeboats" for the crew in case something goes wrong, and they need to leave quickly.

BE A SCIENCE MISSION SPECIALIST

Mission specialists like you are astronauts with expertise in an area of science, medicine, or technology, whose research will advance space exploration.

As a biologist, your mission is to grow green salad vegetables in microgravity. One day, humans will live on the Moon and travel long distances to Mars. They will need to grow their own food, as deliveries from Earth will be infrequent. The ISS is the perfect place to practice all the skills humans need to live off-world. It's time to explore your new home!

The Quest airlock: A hatch used to go outside on a spacewalk.

Columbus laboratory: European research module with controls to clean the air and heat the space station. This is where you are going to work.

The central truss supports all the different parts of the space station.

Robotic arm

Docked crewed USA spacecraft (Dragon)

Unity Node 1: Central corridor, meeting and dining room, and cargo dock.

Harmony Node 2: Houses the controls for the station's power system, plus storage and sleep stations.

Destiny laboratory: US research module with a cycling machine.

Japanese Experiment laboratory: Research module with an airlock, small robotic arm and a storage module.

Equipment and sensors along the truss monitor the space station's orbit, and changes on Earth and in space.

Tranquility Node 3: Gym, toilet, and viewing window.

Today the ISS is as long as a soccer field (356 feet) with a living space larger than a six-bedroom house. The living quarters are made up of modules (rooms) and nodes (connecting corridors).

Zarya: Russian control module and wash station.

Progress: Docked Russian cargo spacecraft.

Soyuz: Docked crewed Russian spacecraft.

Zvezda: Russian module with life support systems and cosmonaut sleep stations.

Nauka: Russian laboratory module.

The solar arrays capture the Sun's energy, turning it into electricity to power the station.

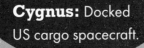

Cygnus: Docked US cargo spacecraft.

29

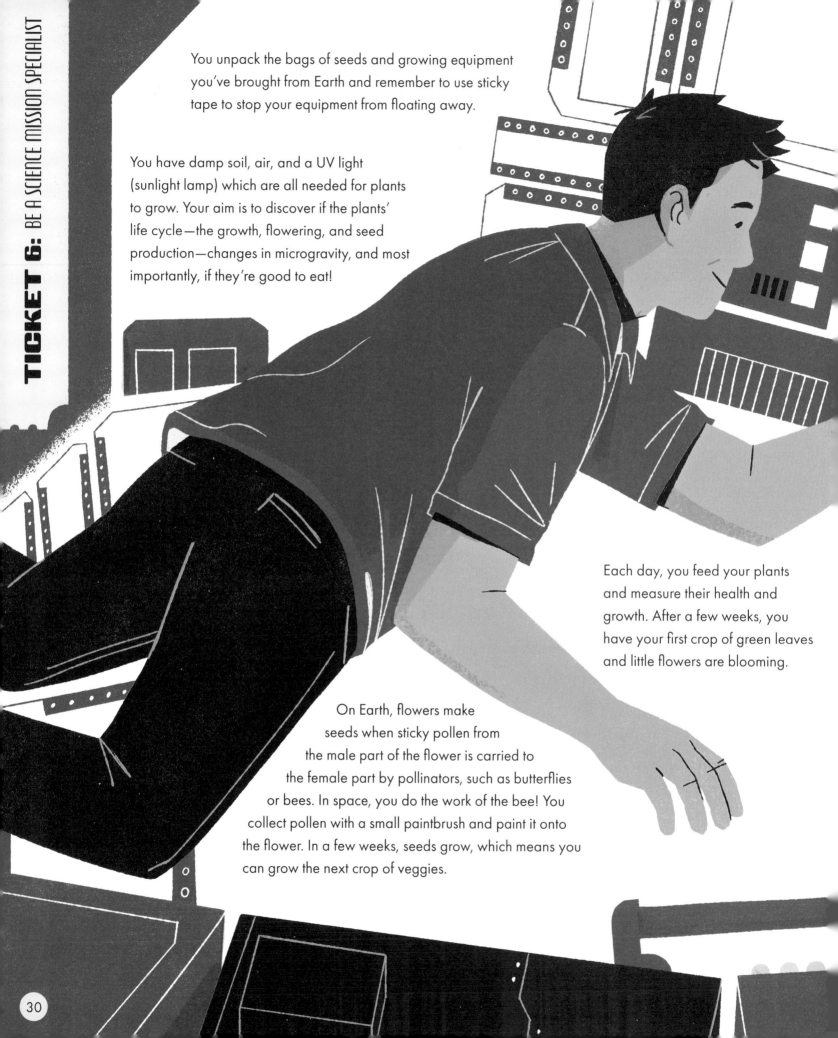

You unpack the bags of seeds and growing equipment you've brought from Earth and remember to use sticky tape to stop your equipment from floating away.

You have damp soil, air, and a UV light (sunlight lamp) which are all needed for plants to grow. Your aim is to discover if the plants' life cycle—the growth, flowering, and seed production—changes in microgravity, and most importantly, if they're good to eat!

Each day, you feed your plants and measure their health and growth. After a few weeks, you have your first crop of green leaves and little flowers are blooming.

On Earth, flowers make seeds when sticky pollen from the male part of the flower is carried to the female part by pollinators, such as butterflies or bees. In space, you do the work of the bee! You collect pollen with a small paintbrush and paint it onto the flower. In a few weeks, seeds grow, which means you can grow the next crop of veggies.

You've proved salad grows in space! The crew enjoy adding the crunchy leaves to their dinner. Everyone agrees your veggie garden is a welcome splash of green amongst the artificial equipment on the space station.

Scientists on the ISS have successfully grown wheat, radish, peppers, zucchini, tomatoes, and sunflowers in small batches.

Astronaut food comes in ready-to-heat meals or dehydrated food pouches with all the water removed. Astronauts add water to the dehydrated food from the station water dispenser, mix it with the contents, and suck it up through a straw. The crew also ask their families to send their favorite snacks on the next supply rocket. Astronauts have a lot of fun at mealtimes catching blobs of floating food with their mouths.

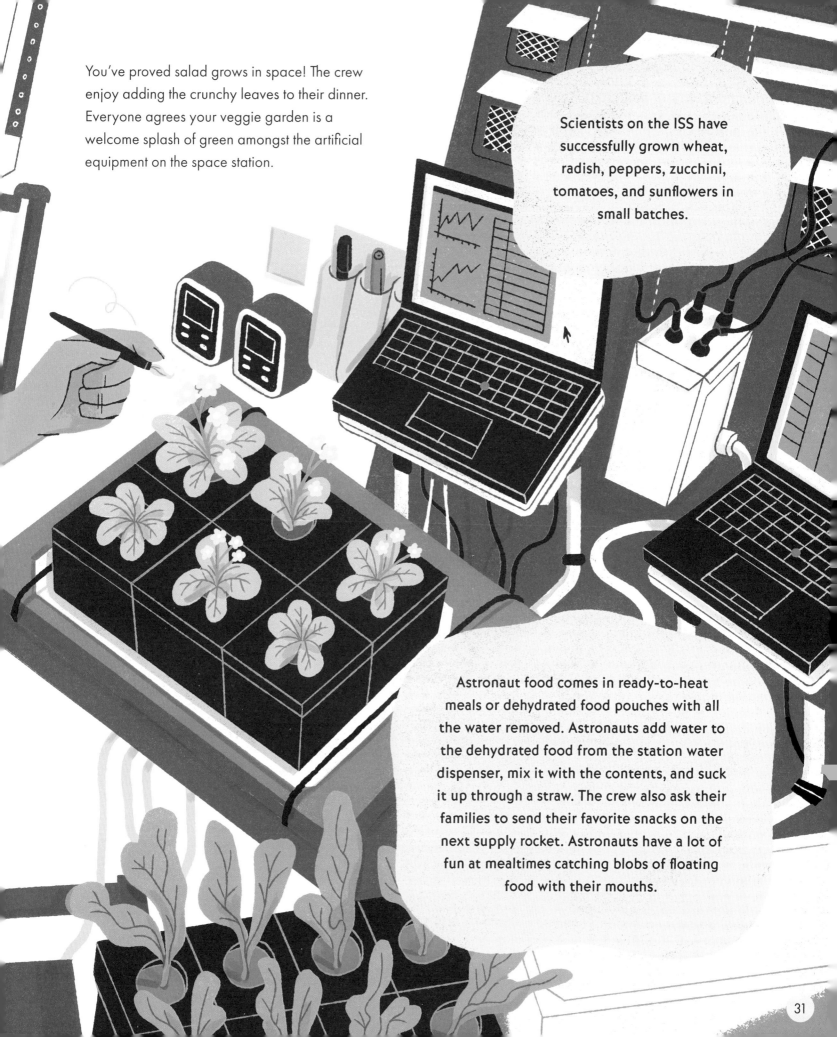

FIND A SPONSOR FOR YOUR SEAT

You can't believe you have made it to the ISS. You aren't a pilot, scientist, or engineer: you are an artist, and there haven't been many of those in space. When a space company invited people to put their name forward to win a trip to space, you sent them a drawing. They loved your art imagining how people would live in space! They invited you to live for two weeks on the ISS, and draw ideas for the space hotels of the future.

As you explore the station, you see electrical systems, science experiments, and cargo take up nearly every available space. The ISS is a busy orbiting laboratory and there isn't room for more scientists, let alone space tourists, and it isn't built to be comfortable.

MISSION STATS

Launch vehicle height: 170 feet

Mission type: Low Earth orbit on board the ISS

Altitude: 211 miles

Level of atmosphere: Thermosphere

Time spent in space: Fourteen days

Ticket cost: Zero! Your seat has been sponsored by a company.

The ISS orbits Earth sixteen times a day. The path of the orbit shifts west each time due to the revolution of Earth, so there is a constantly changing view and sixteen sunrises and sunsets.

Your favorite place on the ISS is the cupola viewing window, with its spectacular views of Earth. When you look down, there are no borders between countries, and the browns, greens, and blues of the land and sea are all connected. Earth is one big life-support system for every living thing. Any space station of the future needs to have big windows so travelers can enjoy the view and see how precious and extraordinary our planet is.

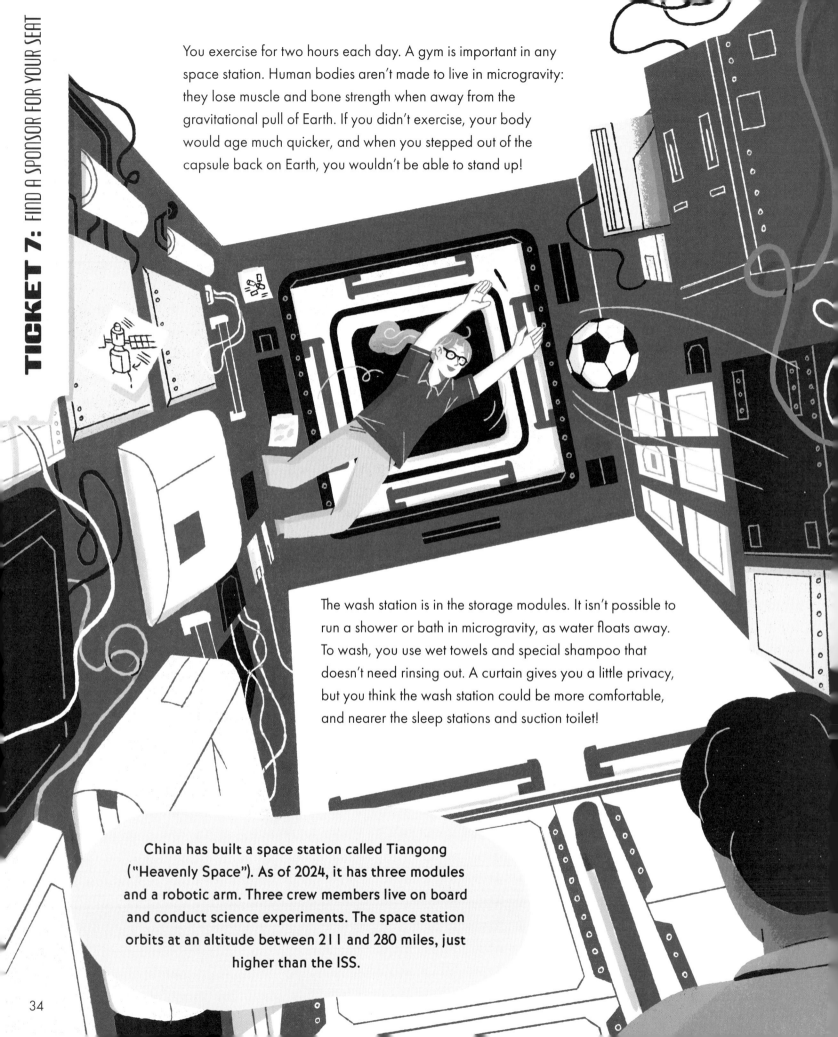

You exercise for two hours each day. A gym is important in any space station. Human bodies aren't made to live in microgravity: they lose muscle and bone strength when away from the gravitational pull of Earth. If you didn't exercise, your body would age much quicker, and when you stepped out of the capsule back on Earth, you wouldn't be able to stand up!

The wash station is in the storage modules. It isn't possible to run a shower or bath in microgravity, as water floats away. To wash, you use wet towels and special shampoo that doesn't need rinsing out. A curtain gives you a little privacy, but you think the wash station could be more comfortable, and nearer the sleep stations and suction toilet!

China has built a space station called Tiangong ("Heavenly Space"). As of 2024, it has three modules and a robotic arm. Three crew members live on board and conduct science experiments. The space station orbits at an altitude between 211 and 280 miles, just higher than the ISS.

34

At the end of the day, it's time to relax and have some fun. You play space soccer with the crew and then show off your microgravity gymnastics. You also video chat with friends and space fans on Earth. When you post your new drawings on social media they are shared around the world, creating a buzz about space travel and humankind's future amongst the stars.

The ISS is expected to operate until at least 2030 when NASA is planning to replace it with a new station. Space companies are working together to construct new modules and life-support systems. New modules are attached to the ISS and tested for safety before they are used to build a new station.

In the future, NASA also plans to build a Moon-orbiting space station to study the Moon and assist with lunar landings.

WORK AS A SPACE ENGINEER

**Ever since you were little, you wanted to understand how machines worked.
You became an aerospace engineer and learnt how to build and repair
spacecraft. This is your first trip to space and you're excited to join the ISS crew.
Your mission is to replace the space station's rechargeable batteries.
The only way to do that is to go on a spacewalk. *So, time to suit up!***

You wear absorbent pants (there are no toilet stops in space) and pull on your under-suit —a onesie that pipes cool water around your body to prevent overheating. The crew help you put on your spacesuit and make sure everything is airtight. Your spacesuit is a human-sized spacecraft.

You must sit and breathe pure oxygen for two hours before you go outside so your body can cope with the lower air pressure in your suit. This enables you to stay outside for longer and stops your suit from blowing up like a balloon. Astronauts always spacewalk in pairs. You talk through the mission and check your tool belts. Finally, you're good to go.

Your EVA suit

A spacewalk is also called an EVA—extra-vehicular activity. EVA suits are much more advanced than the spacesuits astronauts wear to take off and land. They have at least sixteen layers of cooling, insulating, airtight, tearproof, fireproof, dustproof, reflective materials to keep the astronaut safe.

Helmet: features a wide-angle gold-coated visor (to reflect the Sun's glare), voice-activated display, multi-way communications, camera and night lights.

Hard upper torso (HUT): a control panel, shoulder cameras, and colored stripes (so each astronaut can be recognized).

Portable life-support system: a battery power source that keeps the suit pressurized, circulates breathable air, removes poisonous CO_2 gas and pipes water from a tank for cooling and drinking.

Gloves: with built-in heating and flexible fingers.

SAFER: Simplified Aid for EVA Rescue—a jet pack in case an untethered astronaut drifts away from the space station.

Lower torso: with rings at the waist to tether a spacewalker to the space station and to attach tools.

MISSION STATS

Launch vehicle height: 170 feet

Mission type: Low Earth orbit on board the ISS

Altitude: 211 miles

Level of atmosphere: Thermosphere

Time spent in space: 182 days

Ticket cost: Zero! You are paid by a space company to repair spacecraft in orbit.

You move into the airlock chamber and the crew seal the hatch behind you. The air is sucked into space and the outer hatch opens.

Woah! The view is awesome and scary. Only the glass in your visor is separating you from the galaxy and you feel very small. You tell yourself to focus and attach a safety tether to a hook on the outside of the space station. You use the numbered handholds to pull yourself up and along the central truss to the battery storage. The space station has a robotic arm. A large box called a pallet is already attached to the arm and contains the new batteries. The crew inside the station move the arm near to where you are going to work.

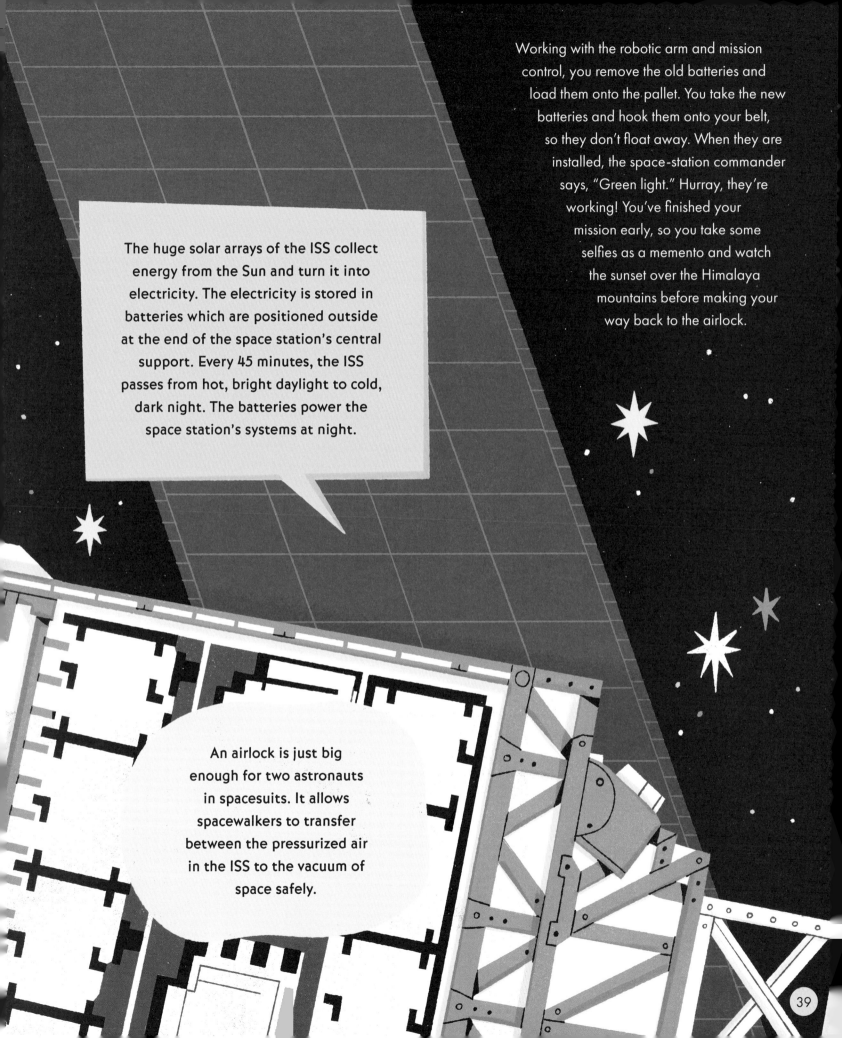

Working with the robotic arm and mission control, you remove the old batteries and load them onto the pallet. You take the new batteries and hook them onto your belt, so they don't float away. When they are installed, the space-station commander says, "Green light." Hurray, they're working! You've finished your mission early, so you take some selfies as a memento and watch the sunset over the Himalaya mountains before making your way back to the airlock.

The huge solar arrays of the ISS collect energy from the Sun and turn it into electricity. The electricity is stored in batteries which are positioned outside at the end of the space station's central support. Every 45 minutes, the ISS passes from hot, bright daylight to cold, dark night. The batteries power the space station's systems at night.

An airlock is just big enough for two astronauts in spacesuits. It allows spacewalkers to transfer between the pressurized air in the ISS to the vacuum of space safely.

ROCKET HALL OF FAME

These rockets and spacecraft are designed to carry people into space. The greater the distance to travel, the bigger the rocket must be to carry fuel, cargo, and people out of Earth's atmosphere and on to their destination. Usually, only a few astronauts launch at a time in a small spacecraft or capsule attached to a rocket. As of 2024, Starship is the largest rocket ever built. At launch, it's about as tall as a forty-storey building! It is designed to transport up to one hundred people to the Moon or even Mars.

The Space Shuttle was the first reusable spacecraft. Between 1981 and 2011, five Space Shuttles carried more than 800 astronauts into space on 135 missions, which included launching the Hubble space telescope and building the ISS.

Soyuz means "union" in Russian and is the longest-running human spacecraft program.

Spica rocket	**SpaceShip2**	**New Shepard**	**Soyuz**	**Atlas 5 N22 / Starliner**	**STS – Space Shuttle**	**Long March-2F /Shenzhou**
Copenhagen Suborbitals (Denmark)	Virgin Galactic (USA)	Blue Origin (USA)	Roscosmos (Russia)	United Launch Alliance/Boeing (USA)	NASA (USA)	CNSA (China National Space Administration)
In development at time of writing	2019-present	2015-present	1965-present	2019-present	1981-2011	2003-present

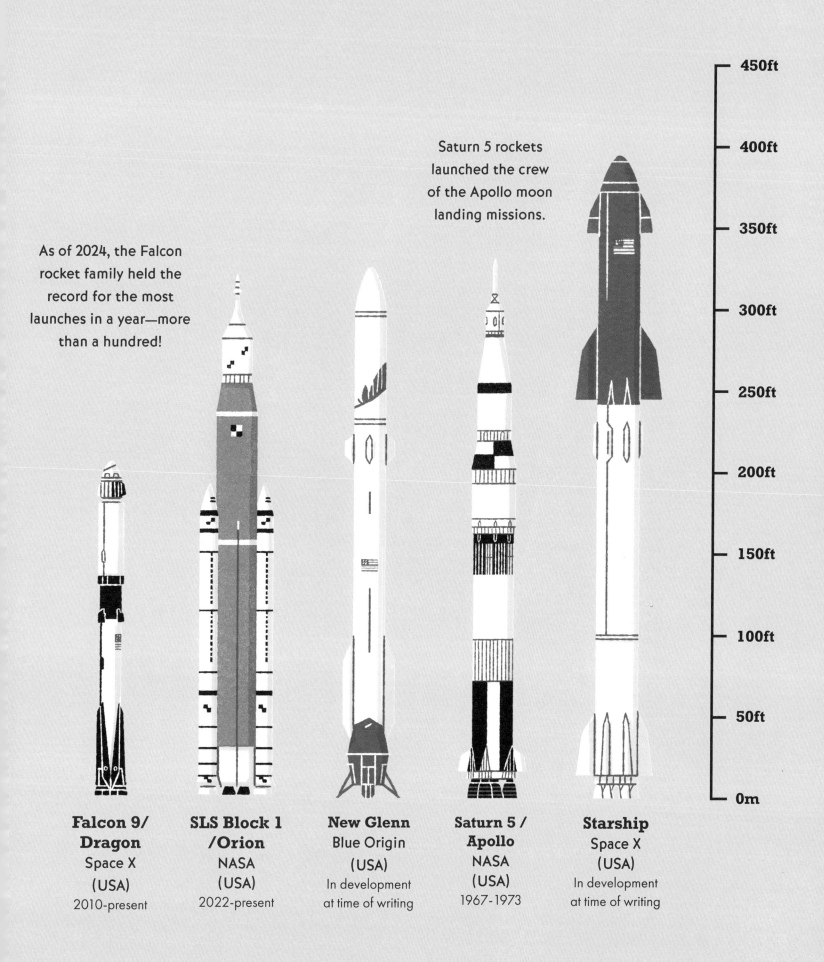

Saturn 5 rockets launched the crew of the Apollo moon landing missions.

As of 2024, the Falcon rocket family held the record for the most launches in a year—more than a hundred!

Falcon 9/ Dragon
Space X
(USA)
2010-present

SLS Block 1 /Orion
NASA
(USA)
2022-present

New Glenn
Blue Origin
(USA)
In development
at time of writing

Saturn 5 / Apollo
NASA
(USA)
1967-1973

Starship
Space X
(USA)
In development
at time of writing

450ft
400ft
350ft
300ft
250ft
200ft
150ft
100ft
50ft
0m

VISIT THE MOON

When a space company announces they can take the first space tourists on a flyby of the Moon, you jump at the chance to go. It's a high-price ticket but a once-in-a-lifetime trip.

You train with the crew for six months. Space travel is risky, and the farther away from Earth you travel, the more dangerous it becomes. But this doesn't put you off—you live for adventure! You will be one of the first people to return to the Moon since Apollo 17 left lunar orbit over 50 years ago.

Thousands of people camp out to watch as you blast into space in the tallest, most powerful rocket ever flown. Once the spaceship is in orbit, the booster separates and returns to Earth. Then the spacecraft fires its engines and heads out of orbit toward the Moon. For three days you travel through space, getting used to living in microgravity.

You help the crew monitor the ship's systems and check each other's health. Through the viewing window, the Moon grows larger each day. You enter orbit and see thousands of meteor craters below and the site of the last Moon landing.

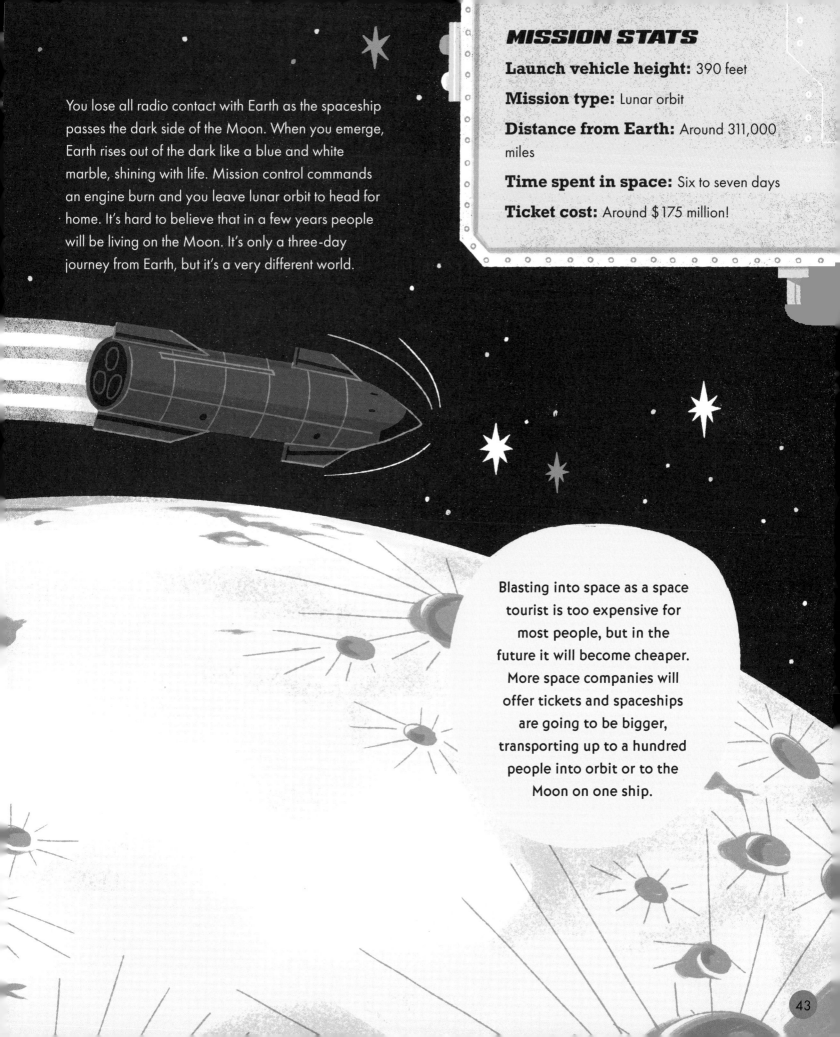

You lose all radio contact with Earth as the spaceship passes the dark side of the Moon. When you emerge, Earth rises out of the dark like a blue and white marble, shining with life. Mission control commands an engine burn and you leave lunar orbit to head for home. It's hard to believe that in a few years people will be living on the Moon. It's only a three-day journey from Earth, but it's a very different world.

MISSION STATS

Launch vehicle height: 390 feet

Mission type: Lunar orbit

Distance from Earth: Around 311,000 miles

Time spent in space: Six to seven days

Ticket cost: Around $175 million!

Blasting into space as a space tourist is too expensive for most people, but in the future it will become cheaper. More space companies will offer tickets and spaceships are going to be bigger, transporting up to a hundred people into orbit or to the Moon on one ship.

NASA's Artemis program plans to return people to the Moon again and again to create an international lunar community. This will include a space station called the lunar gateway, where spacecraft will dock, and a research base where scientists will practice all the skills needed to live off-world.

There's lots of work to do on the Moon. Astronauts will:

✴ Find and study ice in the craters at the south pole and in the regolith (lunar rock).

✴ Experiment with melting and purifying ice to use as a source of air, rocket fuel, and drinking water.

✴ Measure moonquakes and asteroid impacts with a seismograph.

✴ Collect and study rocks to learn about the origins of Earth and our solar system.

✴ Construct a lunar base. NASA and China both have plans to build Moon bases in the 2030s.

What will it be like to live on the Moon?

✳ The surface of the Moon is as hot as 250°F during the day and as cold as -207°F at night, compared to Earth's average temperature of 59°F.

✳ One Moon day and night is 29.5 Earth days. A lunar base would be situated near the south pole which has sunlight most of the time, unlike the equator of the Moon which has two weeks of continuous sunlight followed by two weeks of continuous night.

✳ The Moon has a very thin atmosphere called an exosphere. There is no air to breathe and very little protection from radiation and meteors. A lunar base may need to be partly underground for safety.

✳ Gravity on the Moon is one-sixth of Earth's, which means astronauts can move and jump higher and more easily than they can on Earth.

VOLUNTEER TO COLONIZE MARS

Would you like to be one of the first people to set foot on Mars? By the time you're an adult, the first spaceships will be leaving for our neighboring planet. These missions will need crews of brave explorers with diverse skills to build a colony on Mars. This is the ultimate adventure, and it will guarantee you a spot in the space hall of fame!

You are part of a crew of eight people who have trained together for months. They will be your new Martian family. After launch, the spaceship enters Earth's orbit and docks with a fuel tanker to fill up for the long trip.

MISSION STATS

Launch vehicle height: 394 feet, including 164-foot return vehicle

Mission type: Martian landing

Distance from Earth: An average of 300 million miles

Time spent away from Earth: Around two years

Ticket cost: Zero! You work for a space exploration company.

During the approximately seven-month journey, everyone exercises for at least two hours each day to avoid muscle loss from living in microgravity. When you're not on duty, you wear your VR headset and play programs and games with images of Earth, to stop feeling homesick.

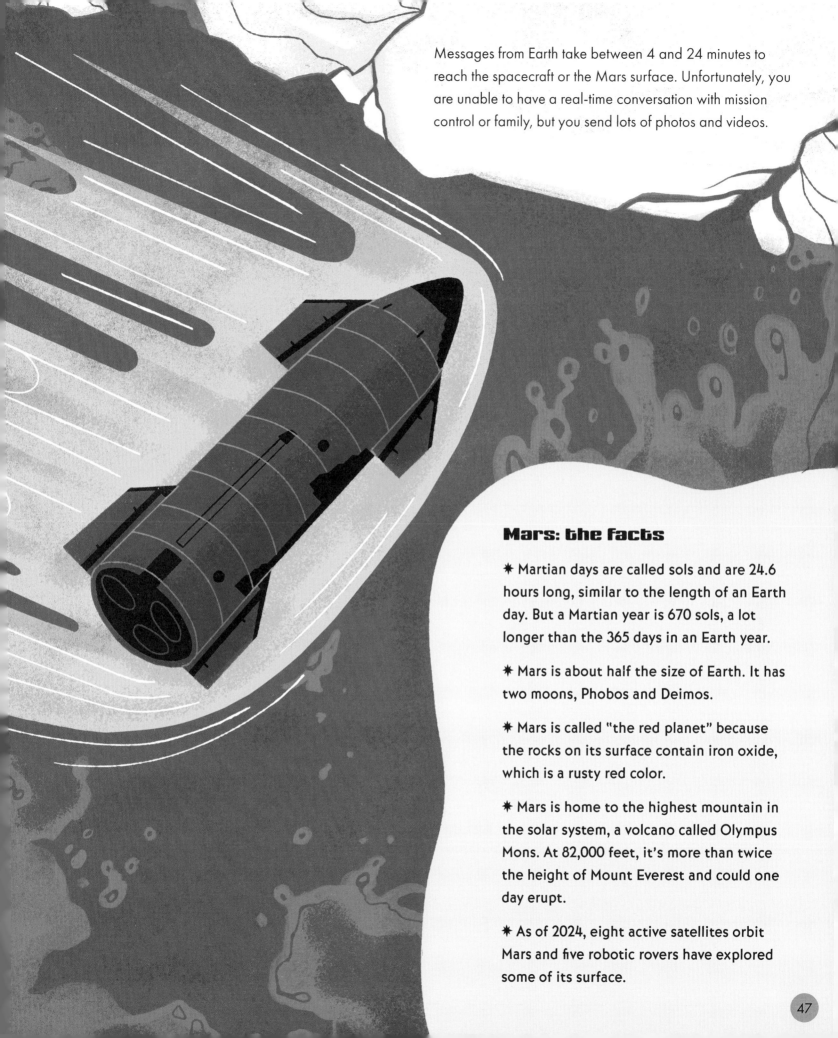

Messages from Earth take between 4 and 24 minutes to reach the spacecraft or the Mars surface. Unfortunately, you are unable to have a real-time conversation with mission control or family, but you send lots of photos and videos.

Mars: the facts

✳ Martian days are called sols and are 24.6 hours long, similar to the length of an Earth day. But a Martian year is 670 sols, a lot longer than the 365 days in an Earth year.

✳ Mars is about half the size of Earth. It has two moons, Phobos and Deimos.

✳ Mars is called "the red planet" because the rocks on its surface contain iron oxide, which is a rusty red color.

✳ Mars is home to the highest mountain in the solar system, a volcano called Olympus Mons. At 82,000 feet, it's more than twice the height of Mount Everest and could one day erupt.

✳ As of 2024, eight active satellites orbit Mars and five robotic rovers have explored some of its surface.

The lander descends, blowing up clouds of red dust, and touches down in a valley that was once a glacial river. Uncrewed cargo ships landed months ago, delivering equipment, robots, food, clothing, and medical supplies, and robotic rovers found ice water nearby. You step outside in your spacesuit and marvel at the empty beauty of Mars.

What will it be like to live on Mars?

✳ Earth and Mars orbit the Sun at different distances and speeds. Every twenty-six months, the two planets come closest together. Every mission to or from Mars must wait for this launch window, when journey time is shortest.

✳ People will need to wear spacesuits to go outside. The atmosphere is very thin and mostly carbon dioxide, which is unbreathable.

✳ The atmosphere does not trap heat, so it can be warm in the day but very cold at night. The average surface temperature is -81°F.

✳ Mars has wispy clouds and winds which sometimes whip up huge dust storms that can cover the whole planet.

✳ Gravity is about one-third of Earth's, which means astronauts can move and jump higher and more easily than they can on Earth.

The crew set about constructing a science outpost. Your mission is to set up a laboratory in the habitat and explore an ancient, dried-up riverbed. Mars was once warmer than it is today, and had rivers that flowed into seas. The big question is: was there once life on Mars? You take samples of ice and rock and return to the lab to look at them under the microscope, hoping to find fossils or signs of tiny microbes.

You haven't found anything yet, but you won't give up. You want to be the first person to discover life on another planet and you only have a few months before the next launch window to return to Earth. Will you stay, or take your rock collection home with you?

LAUNCH A TIME CAPSULE

If you love the idea of traveling amongst the stars but are not so keen on blasting into orbit, then this is the perfect ticket for you. Choose some mementoes about your life on Earth, seal them inside a time capsule, then send them on a rocket into space!

A CubeSat is a satellite about the size of a shoe box, in which small items can be placed. Satellites are launched into space as part of the cargo of an uncrewed rocket. Once the rocket has reached orbit, the cargo doors open and out flies your time capsule satellite. The flight path is controlled from Earth.

MISSION STATS

Satellite size: 12 × 8 × 8 inches

Mission type: You choose!

Distance from Earth: You choose!

Time spent in space: One hundred to one billion years!

Ticket cost: $30,000+, depending on provider and size of capsule

Decisions to make before launch

* Where do you want your capsule to go? Into orbit? Into outer space? To another planet?

* Time capsules are meant to be found in the future. But how far in the future?

* Who would you like to find it? Your family in the future? Someone from a future civilization? An alien from another world?

* The most important part: what are you going to put inside?

Your launch date is approaching! Time to get creative...

Here are some real-life examples of space-traveling time capsules.

In 1977, two deep space probes called Voyager 1 and Voyager 2 were launched. A golden record was placed in each probe as a greeting to anyone that might one day find them. Engraved on the record are instructions showing how to play it, a picture of a man and a woman and a star map showing where the spacecraft came from. It contains images, music, voices, and the sounds of Earth. In 2012 Voyager 1 left our solar system, followed by Voyager 2 in 2018. The probes continue their journey into interstellar space. Voyager 1 is Earth's farthest-flying spacecraft.

Many civilizations have come and gone through the ages, their history buried or eroded by wind and rain. Artist Trevor Paglen believes our civilization will also end one day and others will replace it. He collected one hundred black and white photographs of life on Earth on a disk and sent it on a satellite to a high Earth orbit, where they can safely stay for millions of years, a gift for future historians.

In 2021, an uncrewed spacecraft called Lucy set off to study asteroids near Jupiter. It carries a plaque engraved with a map of its journey and quotes from famous leaders, scientists, authors, songwriters, and poets. Once Lucy's mission is complete, it will continue to orbit the Sun. Far in the future, people can retrieve Lucy, read our messages and learn about the early days of space exploration.

When Gene Roddenberry, the creator of the popular sci-fi series *Star Trek*, died in 1991, his family sent his ashes into space. Gene's family wanted his spirit to forever float toward the far-off worlds that inspired his stories.

SEND A MESSAGE ON A BEAM OF LIGHT

Your class has been invited to write messages which will be beamed across the galaxy on radio waves. One day, your message might be listened to by someone who lives on a distant planet.

When you look up at the night sky, every star you see is a sun and most of these suns have at least one orbiting planet. Could one of these planets support life like Earth does? Perhaps there's an advanced civilization like ours that also uses radio to communicate. It's an exciting idea, and scientists think it's possible.

MISSION STATS

Size of transmitter/receiver dish: 1000-foot diameter

Mission type: First contact

Distance from Earth: Your message will never stop traveling through space!

Time spent in space: Forever!

Ticket cost: Zero! Look out for competitions or become a SETI (search for extra-terrestrial intelligence) scientist.

Your message will be coded by a computer and turned into a radio signal. A giant radio telescope with a transmitter and antenna will send the signal on radio waves toward a group of stars. If a message is sent back to Earth, the radio telescope will capture the radio waves in its large receiving dish and a computer will try to decode the message so it can be read and understood.

Just right

"Goldilocks" planets are not too hot and not too cold, but just right for liquid water to exist, which could support life. One such planet is Earth. Scientists use powerful orbiting observation telescopes to search for other Goldilocks planets in the habitable zone around a star. This is where extra-terrestrial life is most likely to be discovered. Through a telescope, a planet orbiting in front of a star shows as a black dot against the star's bright light. Scientists can calculate the planet's size and orbital path, and sometimes identify gases in its atmosphere.

Radio waves travel at light speed, which is *much* faster than spacecraft can travel. In 1.3 seconds, your message will have passed the Moon. In 30 minutes, it will be approaching Jupiter. In a year and eight months, it will have left Earth's solar system and be on its way to the next one.

Light speed

Radio waves are a form of light, and light travels at the fastest known speed in the universe. A lightyear is the distance that light can travel in one Earth year. Light travels at 186,000 miles per second. Our fastest spacecraft reach speeds that are only a tiny fraction of the speed of light.

Once transmitted, long-wave radio keeps on moving through space for billions of years. It's like an intergalactic text message.

The Arecibo Message

In 1974, the first radio message was sent toward a distant star cluster to share our existence with any alien civilization that might be able to hear it. The message included a simple picture of a radio telescope and Earth's solar system, a stick figure of a human and facts about life on Earth. The message is still traveling to a cluster of stars 25,000 lightyears away.

Typically, a message might say, *Hi, we're here. Is anyone else out there?* But what else should we say to introduce ourselves? Imagine if you received a message from an alien world. What would you like to know about their life and where they live? And what message would you send back?

Space is BIG!

There are eight planets orbiting our sun—Mercury, Venus, Earth, Mars, Jupiter, Saturn, Uranus, and Neptune. Together, they make up our solar system, part of the Milky Way galaxy. There are about 200 billion other solar systems in the Milky Way. Scientists have only studied around 3,500 solar systems through space telescopes so far. No alien signals have been detected, but there's a lot of sky left to watch and listen to!

STEP INTO THE FUTURE OF SPACE

Many space exploration missions are planned for the coming years and decades.
Let's find out what the future holds!

1-10 years in the future

Rockets launch from new spaceports all over the world. Tens of thousands of satellites are orbiting Earth, the Moon, and Mars. Laser communications keep everyone connected. Infrared lasers are better than radio messages at beaming data from relay stations across the solar system to spacecraft and colonies.

1-25 years in the future

Scientists and space tourists visit orbiting space stations and travel to the Moon and Mars to live and work in off-world colonies. Robots such as NASA's Europa Clipper explore Jupiter's moons. Beneath the icy surface of Europa scientists think there is a vast ocean of water or slushy ice that was melted by underwater volcanoes. Animals have been found living near underwater volcanoes on Earth—could there be life in Europa's seas?

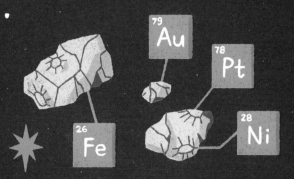

15-30 years in the future
Robots arrive at a nearby asteroid to survey and mine valuable metals needed to build machines and equipment on Earth and in the new colonies.

20-40 years in the future
Surface-to-orbit elevators are constructed. On the Moon, a cable attached to the ground rises through the thin atmosphere to a space station. Solar-powered lifters push a capsule up the cable into orbit. On Earth, a space elevator is also being built. Rockets will no longer be the only way to reach orbit.

40-80 years in the future
A swarm of nano-spacecraft light-sail to nearby solar systems to explore Goldilocks planets and their suns. A powerful laser beam from Earth hits the light-sails and pushes the spacecraft to twenty per cent the speed of light. The nano-spacecraft take 20 years to arrive at our neighboring solar system, Alpha Centauri, and send back data.

GET READY FOR YOUR TICKET TO SPACE!

It's never too early to start practicing the skills needed to travel and live in space. Why not start today?

Go on a roller coaster ride to experience g-forces

Practice living in an enclosed space

Collect rocks and use tools wearing gloves and a helmet

Try a VR simulator

Practice a splash-down landing

Draw or build your own rocket, space station, or lunar base

Listen out for space news

Watch live launches and landings online

Visit a space museum to find out more about space

Camp out beneath the stars

Never give up on your dream to one day fly toward the stars!

"Remember to look up at the stars and not down at your feet. Try to make sense of what you see and wonder about what makes the universe exist. Be curious."

—**Stephen Hawking, physicist and cosmologist**

"Space travel made me feel I have a personal obligation to be a good steward of our planet and to educate others about what's happening to it."

—**Chris Hadfield, astronaut**

"Space is for everybody. It's not just for a few people in science or math, or for a select group of astronauts. That's our new frontier out there, and it's everybody's business to know about space."

—**Christa McAuliffe, teacher and Space Shuttle Challenger astronaut**

Resources for readers, parents and teachers

Space agency websites:

www.nasa.gov/kidsclub/index.html

spaceplace.nasa.gov/

www.esa.int/kids/en/home

Track when the ISS passes near you:

spotthestation.nasa.gov/tracking_map.cfm

Live star-map:

stellarium-web.org

Smithsonian National Air and Space Museum:

airandspace.si.edu

GLOSSARY

absorbent Able to soak up liquid

aerospace The science of airplanes and space flight

altitude Height above sea level

asteroid A rock, smaller than a planet, that orbits the Sun

astronaut A person who is trained to go to space

automated Controlled by machines with little to no input from humans

capsule A small container or spacecraft

CO_2 Carbon dioxide, a gas made of carbon and oxygen

colony A settlement built somewhere by people from somewhere else

to coast To move without using power

curvature The state of being curved

engineer A person who builds, designs, or repairs machines and structures

flammable Able to be easily set on fire

gravity The force that pulls objects toward each other. Earth's gravity keeps you on the planet's surface.

hull The main body of a space vessel, airplane, ship, or other vehicle

infrared Relating to light that has a longer wavelength than red light, making it invisible to human eyes

jet pack A device worn like a backpack that can propel the wearer through space

laser A device that creates a strong beam of light

launch pad A platform from which a rocket can be launched

lunar Relating to the Moon

mesosphere The layer of Earth's atmosphere 164,000-279,000 feet high

meteor A lump of rock or ice from outer space that enters Earth's atmosphere

mission A space flight with a specific goal

mission control The team of people on Earth who oversee a space flight

NASA National Aeronautics and Space Administration, the USA's space agency

orbit The path an object takes around a point in space. To orbit is to follow that path.

parachute A piece of fabric that fills with air to slow down the object or person to which it is attached

pressurized Having pressure that is maintained at a certain level

to purify To remove unwanted substances from something

radiation Energy that travels in the form of particles or waves

robotic Relating to robots, machines that can do jobs by themselves

rocket A vehicle that moves upward by burning fuel to provide thrust

runway A strip of hard, flat ground on which aircraft take off and land

satellite A natural or artificial object that orbits a planet

scuba Self-Contained Underwater Breathing Apparatus, the equipment that allows people to breathe oxygen underwater

seismograph A device that measures the duration and strength of earthquakes

simulator A machine that creates a virtual version of a real-life situation, often used for training pilots and astronauts

software The data and programs that make a computer function

solar system The eight planets, including Earth, and other bodies that orbit the Sun

spaceport An area used for launching spacecraft into space

spacewalk An activity carried out by an astronaut in space, outside their spacecraft

splashdown The landing of a spacecraft in the ocean

stratosphere The layer of Earth's atmosphere 49,000-164,000 feet high

suborbital Relating to the flight of an object that does not complete one orbit of the planet it was launched from

to taxi To drive along the ground before take-off or after landing

telescope A device that makes far-away objects appear closer

thermosphere The layer of Earth's atmosphere 279,000-1,967,000 feet high

troposphere The layer of Earth's atmosphere 0-39,000 feet high

vacuum An area with nothing in it

VR Virtual reality, technology that allows users to interact with digital worlds

For Jack, whose fascination with spacecraft inspired this book. – K. P.

To all those who have ever gazed at the stars in wonder. – T. P.

12 Ways to Get a Ticket to Space © 2024 Quarto Publishing plc.
Text © 2024 Kate Peridot. Illustrations © 2024 Terri Po.

First published in 2024 by Wide Eyed Editions, an imprint of The Quarto Group.
100 Cummings Center, Suite 265D, Beverly, MA 01915, USA.
T +1 978-282-9590 www.Quarto.com

The right of Kate Peridot to be identified as the author and of Terri Po
to be identified as the illustrator of this work has been asserted by them in accordance
with the Copyright, Designs and Patents Act, 1988 (United Kingdom).

A CIP record for this book is available from the Library of Congress.

ISBN 978-0-7112-8637-5
eISBN 978-0-7112-8990-1

The illustrations were created digitally
Set in Eixample Glaces Contrast 2, Rockwell Nova, Sneakers Pro, Bernhard Gothic URW and Futura PT

Published by Debbie Foy
Commissioned by Claire Grace
Designed by Sasha Moxon
Edited by Alex Hithersay
Art directed by Karissa Santos
Production by Dawn Cameron

Manufactured in Guangdong, China TT062024
9 8 7 6 5 4 3 2 1